DK WORKBOOKS

3rd Grade

Problem Solving

Author Linda Ruggieri

Educational Consultant Daniel Ottalini

Penguin
Random
House

Senior Editor Cécile Landau
Editors Nishtha Kapil, Rohini Deb
US Editor Allison Singer
Project Art Editor Dheeraj Arora
Senior Art Editor Ann Cannings
Art Director Martin Wilson
Producer, Pre-Production Nadine King
Producer Priscilla Reby
DTP Designer Anita Yadav
Managing Editor Soma B. Chowdhury
Managing Art Editor Ahlawat Gunjan

First American Edition, 2016
Published in the United States by DK Publishing
345 Hudson Street, New York, New York 10014

Copyright © 2016 Dorling Kindersley Limited
DK, a Division of Penguin Random House LLC
16 17 18 19 20 10 9 8 7 6 5 4 3 2 1
001–285370–Feb/2016

A catalog record for this book
is available from the Library of Congress.
ISBN: 978-1-4654-4453-0

DK books are available at special discounts when purchased
in bulk for sales promotions, premiums, fund-raising, or
educational use. For details, contact: DK Publishing Special
Markets, 345 Hudson Street, New York, New York 10014
SpecialSales@dk.com

Printed and bound in China.

All images © Dorling Kindersley Limited
For further information see: www.dkimages.com

A WORLD OF IDEAS:
SEE ALL THERE IS TO KNOW

www.dk.com

Contents

This chart lists all the topics in the book. Once you have completed each page, stick a star in the correct box below.

★ Place Value

Learn about place value in numbers with up to four digits.

Write the place value of the underlined digit in each number.

6,3_76   h   4,201   t

8,2_89   +   2,254   o

Write these numbers as numerals.

Five thousand two hundred three   5,203

One thousand one hundred thirty-two   1,132

Six hundred two   602

Four thousand two hundred twenty-six   4,226

Seven hundred five   705

Write these numerals as number words.

565   five hundred sixty five

908   nine hundred eight

3,457   three thousand four hundred

9,389   nine thousand three hundred eight nine

7,691   seven thousand six hundred nine one

$x ÷ % = $ + ? − x ÷ % = $? + − % x ÷ = $ + ? − x ÷ %

Practice identifying place value.

Last summer, the baseball teams from every school in the Sun City district got together and played against each other. The scores are shown on the chart below.

Teams	Score (Number of Hits)
Sun City East	14
Sun City North	7
Sun City West	3
Sun City South	11

How many hits did the school teams score altogether? 35

In this number, what digit is in the ones place? 5

How many hits did Sun City East and Sun City West score altogether? Write the answer.

 17

In this number, what digit is in the

ones place? 7

tens place? 10

Multiply the total number of hits scored by 10. Write the answer.

 3.50

In this number, what digit is in the

ones place? 0

tens place? 5

hundreds place? 3

$3   fiftyseven

Learn to identify the operation needed to solve a problem.

Jaiden and his family have recently moved to San Francisco.
Read each problem below. First name the operation needed to solve it.
Then write the number sentence you would use and the answer.

Today, the temperature in San Francisco is 64°F. The weather forecast
for tomorrow predicts it will be 11°F warmer. What will the temperature
be tomorrow?

_____A_____   64 + 11 = 75

Jaiden and his sister Natalie walk to school, which is only four blocks away.
Their neighbor Paul takes a bus to his school, which is 20 blocks away. How
many more blocks than Jaiden and Natalie does Paul travel to school?

_____−_____   20 − 4 = 16 blocks

Jaiden and Natalie go for a swim. The water temperature of the pool is 83°F.
It has gone up 10°F since yesterday. What was the temperature yesterday?

_____A_____   83 + 10 = 93

Mom wants to plant basil and tomatoes in the garden. She has space for
40 rows of plants. She plants 12 rows of basil. How many rows of tomatoes
can she plant?

_____−_____   40 − 12 = 28 rows

Dad, however, wants to plant ten rows of corn, seven rows of parsley,
and three rows of mint. How many rows is this altogether?

_____A_____   10 + 7 + 3 = 20 rows

Add or Subtract?

Practice identifying the correct operation to solve a problem.

Mary, José, and David take lessons at the same music school.
Read each problem below and name the operation needed to solve it.
Then write the number sentence you would use and the answer.

Mary lives seven blocks from the music school. David lives 11 more
blocks away. How many blocks from the school does David live?

.... $\left(\right)$ = $\left(\right)$ blocks

José had $12 when he left the house to go to music school.
He paid $3 bus fare. How much money does he have left?

.... $\left(\right)$ = $\left(\right)$

Mary's lesson lasts 40 minutes. It takes her 10 minutes to reach the school
and the same amount of time to walk home. Altogether, how long does
Mary spend traveling and having her lesson?

.... $\left(\right)$ = $\left(\right)$ minutes

David's lesson also lasts 40 minutes. He takes a bus to and from the
music school. Each trip takes 20 minutes. How many minutes in all
does it take for David's lesson and his ride to and from the school?

.... $\left(\right)$ = $\left(\right)$ minutes

Their music teacher has a total of 25 students. Ten of them take
lessons on Wednesdays. The rest take lessons on Thursdays.
How many students take lessons on Thursdays?

.... $\left(\right)$ = $\left(\right)$ students

GOAL

Learn to solve problems using multiple operations.

Ava went to the movies with her dad. Read each of the problems below. Then figure out the answers, writing out the number sentences you use in the boxes given below. **Hint:** Each problem has two steps.

Ava counted 157 people in the theater at the start of the movie. Ten people came in after it started. At intermission, Ava saw 12 people leave. How many people remained in the theater?

people

Ava waited in line to buy popcorn. There were four people ahead of her and five behind her. How many people in all were waiting in line? If each person took two minutes to buy popcorn, how long did Ava have to wait for her turn?

people

minutes

The popcorn made Ava thirsty. Her dad gave her $5 to buy two bottles of water. One bottle cost $2. How much did Ava pay for two bottles? How much change did she receive?

Ava then saw a pack of her favorite cookies. They cost $8. If Ava had two dollars, how much more money would she need to buy the cookies? If she bought fruit chews for a dollar instead, how much change should she expect?

Practice solving addition and subtraction problems.

Figure out the answers to these problems.

In Brandon's school, there are 137 girls and 250 boys altogether in 2nd and 3rd grade. There are also 100 girls and 104 boys in 4th grade. How many children in 2nd, 3rd, and 4th grades attend Brandon's school?

children

A bus driver picks up 13 people at the first stop, 22 people at the second stop, and 23 people at the third stop. How many passengers are now on the bus?

passengers

Ebony is reading a 378-page book. On the first day, she read 95 pages. On the second day, she read 56 pages. How many pages does she have left to read?

pages

People are waiting by the pier for a ferry. There are 180 people on the left side of the pier and 231 on the right side. How many people are waiting for the ferry altogether?

people

Thirty children have signed up for baseball tryouts. If the coach schedules 12 children for the first day of tryouts and 12 children for the second day, how many children will the coach need to schedule for the third day?

children

★ Multiply by 2 & 3

Learn to solve problems using the 2x and 3x tables.

Figure out the answers to these problems.

Leo has twice as many blue shirts as red shirts. If Leo has three red shirts, how many blue shirts does he have?

⬚ blue shirts

Leo's puppy Skippy eats two cans of food a day. How many cans of food does Skippy eat in a week?

⬚ cans

There are ten tables in Leo's classroom. Each table has two activities on it. How many activities are there altogether in the classroom?

⬚ activities

Figure out the answers to these problems.

A pair of socks costs $3. Maria wants three pairs. How much money does she need to buy them?

⬚

Maria decides to bake cookies for three of her friends. She wants to give four cookies to each of them. How many cookies does she need to bake?

⬚ cookies

Maria spends three days a week on a school project. It takes her five weeks to complete it. How many days does Maria spend on the project altogether?

⬚ days

$\times \div \% = \$ + ? - \times \div \% = \$? + - \% \times \div = \$ + ? - \times \div \%$

Learn to solve problems using the 4x and 5x tables.

Figure out the answers to these problems.

Scarlet is learning to play the violin. She has four lessons a month. How many lessons does she have in a year?

lessons

Scarlet and four of her friends sell tickets for a school concert. They sell four tickets each. How many tickets do they sell between them?

tickets

Scarlet plays her violin at the concert. She and the other musicians sit in four rows on the stage. There are eight musicians in each row. How many musicians are there altogether?

members

Figure out the answers to these problems.

Lydia collects teddy bears. She started her collection with six teddy bears, but now has five times that number. How many teddy bears does she have?

teddy bears

Lydia then decides to share her teddy bears with her five cousins. She gives each cousin two bears. How many teddy bears does she give away?

teddy bears

Lydia displays some of her remaining teddy bears on three shelves, with five bears on each shelf. How many bears does she put on display?

teddy bears

GOAL

Learn that numbers you multiply together are called **factors**, and the answer this gives is called the **product**.

$$6 \quad x \quad 3 \quad = \quad \boxed{18}$$

factor x factor = product

Find the missing factor to complete these multiplication equations.

$\boxed{4}$ x 6 = 24   5 x $\boxed{9}$ = 45 $\boxed{10}$ x 5 = 50   8 x $\boxed{3}$ = 24

3 x $\boxed{7}$ = 21 $\boxed{}$ x 4 = 48   3 x $\boxed{}$ = 36 $\boxed{}$ x 8 = 40

Anna and Max visit the local art museum. Read each problem below. Then find the missing factor to solve each problem.

Anna and Max see 45 paintings across five rooms of the museum. If each room contains the same number of paintings, how many are there in a room?

$\boxed{}$ paintings

It takes them 18 minutes to look at three exhibits. If they look at each for the same amount of time, how many minutes did they spend per exhibit?

$\boxed{}$ minutes

In the café, Anna counts 40 cupcakes, arranged in four rows. Each row contains the same number of cupcakes. How many cupcakes are there in a row?

$\boxed{}$ cupcakes

Anna buys 20 postcards from the gift shop. This is four times the number of cards that Max buys. How many postcards does Max buy?

$\boxed{}$ postcards

Learn to solve problems using the 6x table.

Figure out the answers to these problems.

Chloe's mom bought six tickets
for a cat show. Each ticket costs $12.
How much did Chloe's mom spend
on tickets?

At the cat show, Chloe saw a booklet with
photos of cats. It cost $6 a copy. Her mom
asked her to buy three copies. How much
did the three booklets cost?

Chloe went to the snack table. A sandwich
cost $4 and a bottle of juice cost $2. She
ordered six sandwiches and six bottles of juice.
How much did she pay?

Chloe looked after her friend's kitten,
Spot, for six days. Spot slept for ten
hours a day. How many hours did
Spot sleep while staying with Chloe?

 hours

Six of Chloe's friends came to visit, and
each one brought two toys for Spot.
How many toys was Spot given?

 toys

GOAL

Learn to solve problems using the 7x table.

Figure out the answers to these problems.

Lynn buys some new socks for her tennis lessons. She buys five pairs. They cost $7 a pair. How much does Lynn pay for the socks?

```
.........
:       :
:       :
.........
```

At the start of their tennis lesson, Lynn and the other students wait in the gym for the teacher to arrive. They sit in three rows. Lynn counts seven students in each row. How many students are in Lynn's tennis class?

```
.........
:       :  students
.........
```

At the end of the class, Lynn and her friend Allie help pick up balls. Lynn picks up seven balls, but Allie picks up twice as many. How many balls does Allie pick up?

```
.........
:       :  balls
.........
```

While waiting for her mom to pick them up, Lynn shares a bar of chocolate with her friend. The chocolate is marked into six rows of seven squares. How many squares of chocolate are there in the bar?

```
.........
:       :  squares
.........
```

On the way home, Lynn's mom stops to get gas. She buys 7 gallons. The price of a gallon is $4. How much does Lynn's mom pay for gas?

```
.........
:       :
:       :
.........
```

Learn to solve problems using the 8x table.

Figure out the answers to these problems.

Eight teams compete in a soccer tournament. If there are 11 players on each team, how many players take part in the tournament?

.... players

Eight players on one team need new jerseys. A jersey costs $8. How much is spent on jerseys for the players?

....

One coach orders five soccer balls for his team to practice with. Each ball costs $8. How much does the coach spend on the five balls altogether?

....

One of the teams practices for four hours a day on the eight days leading up to the tournament. How many hours does the team practice altogether?

.... hours

Posters are made to advertise the tournament. Each of the eight teams distributes ten posters. How many posters are distributed altogether?

.... posters

★ Multiply by 9

Learn to solve problems using the 9x table.

Figure out the answers to these problems.

Jean is preparing dinner for nine people. She plans to serve them two fish cakes each. How many fish cakes must she make?

..... fish cakes

Jean's son Christian is nine years old. Christian's dad, Sam, is four times as old as his son. How old is Sam?

..... years old

Christian and eight friends have lunch in the school cafeteria. They eat three slices of pizza each. How many slices do they eat between them?

..... slices

Christian invites eight friends to a sleepover party. Jean makes five pancakes each for Christian and his guests. How many pancakes does Jean make altogether?

..... pancakes

Christian has two pens and nine pencils. His friend Joe has nine times as many pens and three times as many pencils.

How many pens does Joe have?   ..... pens

How many pencils does Joe have?   ..... pencils

Learn to solve problems using the 10x table.

Figure out the answers to these problems.

Ethan collects baseball cards and wants to buy ten more from his friend Jim. Jim asks $2 for each card. How much must Ethan pay Jim for the ten cards?

....

Jim has been collecting baseball cards for four years. In that time, his dad has given him ten rare cards every year as a birthday gift. How many rare cards has Jim's dad given him so far?

.... cards

For Christmas, Jim receives three more cards from his dad. Ethan is also given some baseball cards for Christmas, but he receives ten times as many as Jim. How many cards does Ethan get for Christmas?

.... cards

In January, Jim and Ethan challenge each other to see who can collect the most cards that month. Ethan collects five cards, but Jim collects ten times that number. How many baseball cards does Jim collect in January?

.... cards

Lee and Jake also collect baseball cards. Lee has collected ten new cards a month for two years. Jake has collected ten cards a month, but only for one year. How many baseball cards do they have altogether?

.... cards

Learn to solve problems using the 11x table.

Figure out the answers to these problems.

Grace plays the piano. She has 11 days to prepare for a concert. She plans to practice for three hours a day. How many hours will she practice altogether?

[____] hours

As well as playing on her own, Grace will also play two duets with a violinist. Each duet is 11 minutes long. How long will Grace and the violinist play together?

[____] minutes

Grace buys a small gift for each of the eleven other musicians involved in the concert. Each gift costs $5. How much does Grace spend on the gifts?

[____]

Grace's teacher buys four bouquets to present to the soloists at the concert. Each bouquet is made up of 11 red roses. How many flowers are there in total?

[____] flowers

After the concert, ten of the musicians go out for pizza. Each person pays $11. How much did they pay in total?

[____]

Learn to solve problems using the 12x table.
Remember: A dozen is another way of saying 12.

Figure out the answers to these problems.

Henry lives on a farm. On Monday, he collects a dozen eggs from the hen house. He collects twice that number on Tuesday. How many eggs does he collect on Tuesday?

⬚ eggs

Henry and his friends work six hours a day for 12 days to build a new chicken coop. How many hours in all does it take to finish the chicken coop?

⬚ hours

Henry's dog Summer has five puppies. He buys 12 bags of treats for each puppy. How many bags of treats does he buy?

⬚ bags

Henry's mom bakes four loaves of bread. She cuts each loaf into 12 slices. How many slices of bread does she have?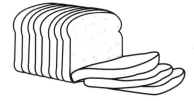

⬚ slices

Henry's sister Callie rides her horse along a trail 12 times. Each trip takes her 10 minutes. How many minutes does she spend riding along the trail altogether?

⬚ minutes

Their parents take Henry and Callie to a horse show. On their way, they stop three times, each time for 12 minutes. How many minutes do they stop altogether?

⬚ minutes

★ More Multiplication

Practice solving problems involving multiplication.

Figure out the answers to these problems.

Anna goes to summer camp for three weeks. She plans to read three books a week while she is away. How many books does she plan to read at camp?

☐ books

The food hall at camp has 11 rows of benches. Each row seats 12 children. How many children can sit in the hall at one time?

☐ children

Some of the older campers set up 6 tents. Each tent has sleeping bags for four children. How many children can sleep in the tents?

☐ children

Anna and five of her friends eat five pancakes each for breakfast. How many pancakes do they eat altogether?

☐ pancakes

At camp, Anna makes seven necklaces using 20 beads in each. What is the total number of beads she uses?

☐ beads

$\times \div \% = \$ + ? - \times \div \% = \$? + - \% \times \div = \$ + ? - \times \div \%$

Learn three key properties of multiplication.

Commutative Property: The product of two numbers is the same regardless of the order of the factors.

$7 \times 6 = 6 \times 7 = 42$

Associative Property: When you multiply three or more numbers, the product is the same regardless of how the factors are grouped.

$(2 \times 6) \times 2 =$
$2 \times (6 \times 2) = 24$

Distributive Property: The sum of two numbers multiplied by a third number is equal to each addend times the third number.

$4 \times 12 = 4 \times (10 + 2) =$
$(4 \times 10) + (4 \times 2) = 48$

Solve the problems below. Then identify which property of multiplication you have used. Write **C** for "commutative property," **A** for "associative property," and **D** for "distributive property."

$(3 \times 6) \times 2 = 3 \times (6 \times 2) = $ ☐ _____

$8 \times 7 = 7 \times 8 = $ ☐ _____

$6 \times 12 = 6 \times (10 + 2) = (6 \times 10) + (6 \times 2) = $ ☐ _____

$9 \times 12 = 12 \times 9 = $ ☐ _____

$(9 \times 3) \times 2 = 9 \times (3 \times 2) = $ ☐ _____

$9 \times 7 = 9 \times (5 + 2) = (9 \times 5) + (9 \times 2) = $ ☐ _____

Learn to divide. The number you are dividing is called the **dividend**. The number you divide by is called the **divisor**. The answer is called the **quotient**.
Remember: You can show division in different ways. For example: $12 \div 4$ is the same as $4\overline{)12}$ with quotient 3.

Dividend → $6 \div 2 = \boxed{3}$ ← Quotient

Divisor (↑ pointing to 2)

Answer each division problem. Then divide the objects shown into sets by circling them to match your answer. The first one has been done for you.

$6 \div 3 = \boxed{2}$

$12 \div 4 = \bigcirc$

$10 \div 2 = \bigcirc$

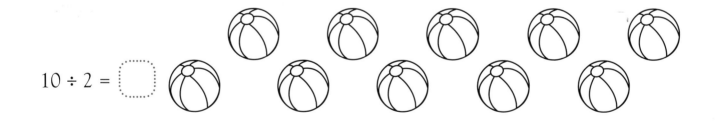

Write the answers. **Hint:** Knowing times tables will help you solve division questions. For example, $2 \times 6 = 12$ will mean $12 \div 6 = 2$ and that $12 \div 2 = 6$.

$6\overline{)12}$ $8\overline{)40}$ $7\overline{)21}$ $7\overline{)77}$

GOAL

Practice division skills.

Write the answers.

$24 \div 4 = \square$ $16 \div 4 = \square$ $36 \div 6 = \square$

$48 \div 4 = \square$ $72 \div 6 = \square$ $56 \div 7 = \square$

$42 \div 7 = \square$ $63 \div 7 = \square$ $36 \div 12 = \square$

$80 \div 10 = \square$ $120 \div 12 = \square$ $100 \div 10 = \square$

Write the answers.

$2\overline{)\,12}$ $5\overline{)\,20}$ $7\overline{)\,49}$ $8\overline{)\,24}$

$9\overline{)\,90}$ $8\overline{)\,48}$ $8\overline{)\,72}$ $11\overline{)\,88}$

★ Division Problems

Learn to solve problems using division.

Figure out the answers to these problems.

Lily and Catherine picked 30 apples. They divided them equally into three baskets. How many apples were in each basket?

[   ] apples

Annie ordered a pizza for her three children. She cut the pizza into eight slices. The children were each given the same number of slices. How many slices did each child receive?

[   ] slices

How many slices of pizza were left for Annie?

[   ] slices

At a sale, a box of eight notepads costs $16. How much would one notepad cost?

[   ]

Bonnie sold 15 bags of candy to five customers. Each customer bought the same number of bags. How many bags did each customer buy?

[   ] bags

Twenty-two students watched a basketball game in the school gym. There were two benches for them to sit on. If ten students could sit on each bench, how many students had to stand?

[   ] students

$ × ÷ % = $ + ? − × ÷ % = $? + − % × ÷ = $ + ? − × ÷ %

Practice solving problems using division.

Students from Parkside High School went out for lunch at the Brew Star Café. Read the menu below. Then figure out the answers to the problems under it. Show the number sentence you use in the box.

Brew Star Café Menu

Hot Dog	$6	Pizza	$5
Meatball Sub	$7	All Drinks	$2

Ella bought one drink each for her students. She paid $22. How many students did she buy drinks for?

_____ students

☐

Six students ordered the same item from the menu. Their bill came to $36. What did the students order? What was the price of that item?

....

☐

Sal placed an order for eight students, who all wanted the same item. The bill came to $56. What did Sal order? What did each one cost?

....

☐

At Nancy's table, three students ordered hot dogs and three ordered pizza. What was the total cost?

☐

Study some common math terms.

s	u	b	t	r	a	c	t	p	d
x	f	j	h	z	f	d	g	r	i
r	a	v	j	z	k	u	s	o	v
u	c	v	m	z	j	q	j	d	i
g	t	v	v	e	h	k	t	u	d
j	o	u	c	r	f	r	s	c	e
k	r	h	x	o	s	o	k	t	n
r	s	p	d	l	u	d	n	r	d
s	e	f	t	i	n	e	d	r	c
q	u	o	t	i	e	n	t	e	e

In the word search puzzle, find and circle the math terms that match each description below. Then write each term next to its description.

To find the difference in value between two numbers. ....

Numbers that are multiplied together. ....

Another name for the answer when multiplying. ....

The product of any number multiplied by 0. ....

A number that is being divided. ....

Another name for the answer when dividing. ....

$\$ \times \div \% = \$ + ? - \times \div \% = \$? + - \% \times \div = \$ + ? - \times \div \%$

Practice finding the correct operation to solve a problem.

Read each problem below and name the operation needed to solve it. Then figure out the answer.

Ted has $42 and Sue has $19. They want to buy a video game to share, which costs $60. Do they have enough money to buy the game?

....

Annette weighs 75 pounds. Her friend Jane weighs 10 pounds less. What does Jane weigh?

....   [ ] pounds

Finley is waiting on line to buy tickets to the zoo. He counts 13 people ahead of him. If each person takes about two minutes to buy tickets, how long will Finley have to wait on line?

....   [ ] minutes

Noah and Danny gather acorns in the park. Noah picks up 44 acorns, but Danny only picks up half as many. How many acorns does Danny pick up?

....   [ ] acorns

Bella takes three of her friends out for ice-cream sundaes. Two girls can share one sundae. How many sundaes does Bella need to buy? A sundae costs $6. How much does Bella spend?

....   [ ] sundaes

....   [ ]

★ More Mixed Problems

Practice solving problems using a variety of operations.

Willie and Jason are at the school book fair. Read each problem below and figure out the answers.

Willie reads four books a month. He wants to buy enough books to last him three months. How many books does he need to buy?

 books

Jason has $20. Most of the books at the fair cost $2 each. Will Jason be able to buy 10 books?

....

Willie buys five biographies for $4 each, and four storybooks for $2 each. Jason buys eight storybooks for $2 each.

How many books do they buy between them?

 books

How much do the books cost altogether?

Mike is planning to sell some baseball cards to buy tickets to a baseball game. Read each problem below and figure out the answers.

Mike sells 20 of his All-Star cards for $3 and 30 of his pitcher cards for $2. How much money does Mike make from selling these cards?

Mike uses some of the money he made to buy three tickets to a baseball game. Each ticket costs $10. How much money does he have left?

At the game, Mike buys a hot dog and a drink. He pays $12.50 for them. How much change does he get from a $20 bill?

$×÷%=$+?—×÷%=$?+—%×÷=$+?—×÷%

Practice solving problems using a variety of operations.

Figure out the answers to these problems.

Aaron is off on vacation for 12 days. He decides to pack two T-shirts for each day away. How many T-shirts does Aaron pack?

☐ T-shirts

There are 22 maple trees in the local park. More trees are being planted today. This will bring the total number of maple trees in the park to 73. How many trees will be planted today?

☐ trees

Joel has 18 nickels in his piggy bank. Steve has three times as many nickels as Joel. How many nickels does Steve have?

☐ nickels

Lisa has 32 balloons. She gives half of them away to her friends Maya and Tim. If she gives them the same number of balloons each, how many balloons do Maya and Tim each receive?

☐ balloons

Alice will be at summer camp for two weeks. She figures that she will need $5 a day spending money while she is there. She already has $60. How much more money does she need?

☐

★ Fractions

Learn that a fraction, such as
$\frac{1}{2}$ (one half) or $\frac{1}{4}$ (one quarter),
is part of a whole.

$\frac{1}{2}$ → 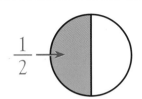 $\frac{1}{4}$ →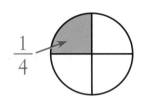

Draw a line from each fraction to the pizza that has that amount shaded.

$\frac{4}{4}$ $\frac{1}{4}$ $\frac{3}{4}$ $\frac{2}{8}$

Fractions can have the same value even if they look different. In each row below, circle the two shapes that have the same fraction shaded.

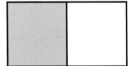   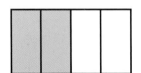   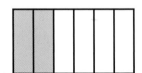

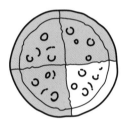   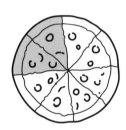   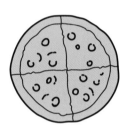   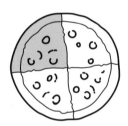

$\$ \times \div \% = \$ + ? - \times \div \% = \$? + - \% \times \div = \$ + ? - \times \div \%$

Practice recognizing fractions of shapes.

Draw a line from each shape to the fraction that matches the shaded part.

$\dfrac{1}{2}$

$\dfrac{1}{4}$

$\dfrac{2}{3}$

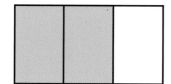

$\dfrac{1}{6}$

The shapes shown below are divided into equal parts. Shade the correct number of parts in each shape to match the fraction above it.

$\dfrac{5}{6}$ $\dfrac{3}{4}$ $\dfrac{1}{2}$

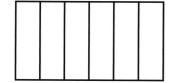

Learn to identify fractions.

The shaded section on each number line below shows a fraction less than 1.
Circle the fraction it represents. The first one has been done for you.

0 ————————→———— 1	$\left(\dfrac{2}{4}\right)$ $\dfrac{2}{3}$
0 —→———————————— 1	$\dfrac{1}{5}$ $\dfrac{1}{8}$
0 ————————→———— 1	$\dfrac{3}{8}$ $\dfrac{4}{8}$

Write the fraction that represents the number of balloons with a pattern
on them in each row. The first one has been done for you.

$\dfrac{2}{4}$

$\dfrac{}{}$

$\dfrac{}{}$

$\$\times\div\%=\$+?-\times\div\%=\$?+-\%\times\div=\$+?-\times\div\%$

Practice identifying fractions.

Write the missing fractions in the boxes along these number lines.

0 [ ] $\frac{2}{10}$ $\frac{3}{10}$ [ ] [ ] $\frac{6}{10}$ [ ] $\frac{8}{10}$ $\frac{9}{10}$ 1

0 $\frac{1}{4}$ [ ] $\frac{3}{4}$ 1 [ ] [ ] $1\frac{3}{4}$ 2

0 $\frac{1}{6}$ $\frac{2}{6}$ [ ] $\frac{4}{6}$ [ ] 1 [ ] [ ] $1\frac{3}{6}$ [ ] $1\frac{5}{6}$ 2

0 $\frac{1}{8}$ [ ] [ ] $\frac{4}{8}$ [ ] [ ] $\frac{7}{8}$ 1

Color in $\frac{2}{5}$ of these fish.

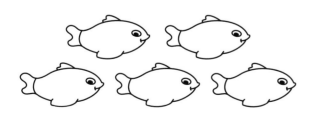

Color in $\frac{4}{8}$ of these rabbits.

Learn to identify **quadrilaterals**. These are 2-D shapes that all have four straight sides and four angles. Squares, rectangles, rhombuses, parallelograms, and trapezoids are all types of quadrilateral.

Draw lines to match each quadrilateral on the left to its description on the right.

A **rectangle** has opposite sides that are the same length. Its angles are all right angles.

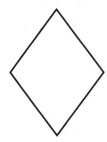

A **square** has sides that are all the same length. Its angles are all right angles.

A **trapezoid** has one pair of opposite sides that are parallel.

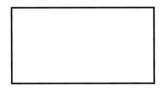

A **rhombus** has sides that are all the same length. Opposite angles are equal, but are not right angles.

A **parallelogram** has two pairs of opposite sides that are parallel.

$x ÷ % = $ + ? — x ÷ % = $? + — % x ÷ = $ + ? — x ÷ %

Practice identifying 3-D shapes. **Remember:** 3-D shapes are solid shapes that have three dimensions—width, height, and depth. They have flat and curved surfaces, known as faces.

Draw lines to match each 3-D shape to its description.

A **cone** has one flat face and one curved face.

A **cylinder** has two flat faces and one curved face.

A **cube** has six flat, square faces that are all the same size.

A **triangular-based pyramid** has four flat triangle-shaped faces.

A **sphere** has one continuous curved face.

A **triangular prism** has five faces, two triangular and three that are either square or rectangular.

★ Measuring Length

Practice measuring length, using both inches and centimeters.

How long are these items? First use a ruler marked in inches to measure them. Then use a ruler marked in centimeters. **Note:** Remember to put either **in** (for inches) or **cm** (for centimeters) as part of your answer.

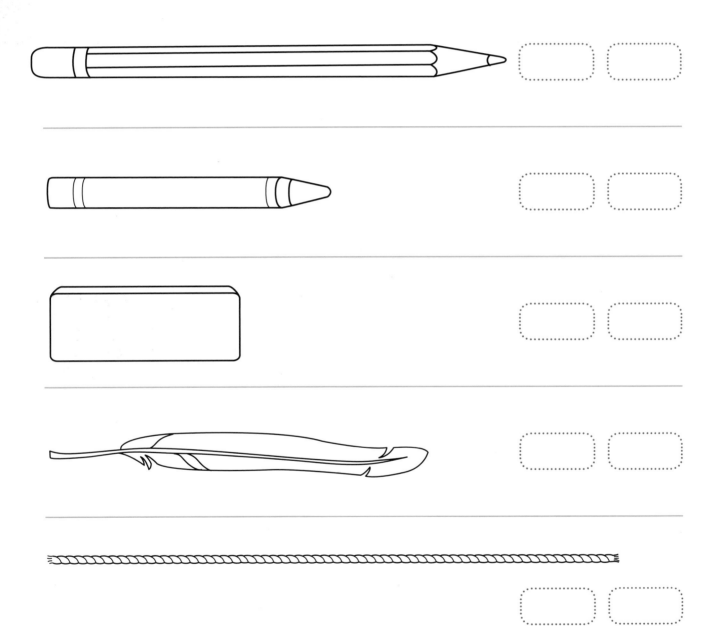

$\$\times\div\%=\$+?-\times\div\%=\$?+-\%\times\div=\$+?-\times\div\%$

Learn to calculate perimeters. **Note:** The perimeter of a shape is the distance around its outer edge. For example:

6 m

5 m |￣￣￣￣| 5 m

6 m

Perimeter of rectangle =

6 m + 5 m + 6 m + 5 m = ⟨ 22 m ⟩

Now solve these problems.

Sarah ordered a cake that was 30 cm long and 15 cm wide. What was its perimeter?

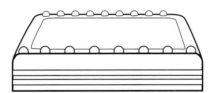

The length of a swimming pool measures 7 m, and its width measures 5 m. What is the perimeter of the pool?

The perimeter of a fenced yard is 40 ft. If its length is 12 ft, what is its width?

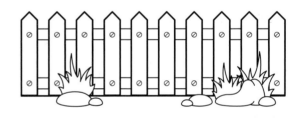

Malala is making a poster for her social studies project. The poster is 2 ft by 3 ft. What is its perimeter?

Suki is buying some ribbon to make a border for a bulletin board. The bulletin board is 10 ft by 5 ft.

What length of ribbon does she need to make the border?

If the ribbon Suki wants costs $2 a foot, how much does Suki need to spend?

GOAL

Learn to measure the area of a 2-D shape. **Note:** The area of a shape is the amount of space it covers. You can measure area using squares. Each square is a square unit. For example:

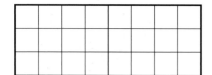

Area of the rectangle = 24 square units
or (8 x 3) square units
or **length** x **width**

Figure out the answers to these problems.

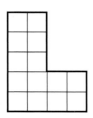

The school playground is shaped like the letter L. What is its area in square units?

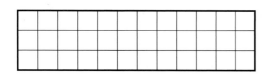

The camp swimming pool is 12 m long and 3 m wide. What is the area of the pool?

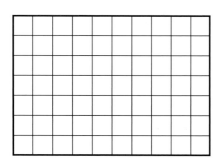

Julio's math book is 10 in by 7 in. What is the area of his math book?

Mass & Volume Problems

Learn to solve problems about mass and volume.

Figure out the answers to these problems.

Sal is making waffles with his mom. The recipe says to use 1 cup of milk to make a batch of 10 waffles. How much milk must Sal and his mom use to make 20 waffles?

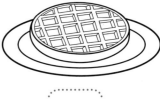

.... cups

Mabel puts 2 liters of lemonade in a jug. She drinks half of it, then her friend drinks half of what's left. How much lemonade is still in the jug?

....

Kim needs 3 kg of flour to make cupcakes for her sister's birthday party. At the store, a bag of flour weighs 2 kg. How many bags of flour must she buy to make sure she has enough for the cupcakes?

Sam and Peter are packing for a trip to the UK. The airline's website says the luggage allowance per person is 40 kg. When packed, Sam's bag weighs 38 kg, but Peter's weighs 46 kg.

How much must Peter reduce the weight of his luggage by for it to be allowed on the plane?

What weight of the luggage that Peter must remove from his bag can be carried in Sam's bag?

What weight of Peter's luggage must he leave behind?

Learn words and phrases that refer to the number of minutes when telling the time. For example:

twenty to three

ten past twelve

Write these times as they would appear on a digital clock.

quarter to ten

twenty to eight

half past six

ten past five

Solve each of these problems. First write the time as it would appear on a digital clock, then draw the hands in the correct position on the analog clock.

This afternoon, Lily started her homework at ten past five. What time did the clock show?

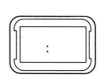 

Anna is fifteen minutes late for a doctor's appointment, scheduled for twenty-five past four. What time is it?

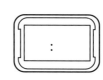 

Tim's party started at half past one. Two of his friends arrived half an hour early. What time did they arrive?

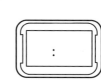 

$×÷%=$+?−×÷%=$?+−%×÷=$+?−×÷%

Learn to solve problems about time.

Solve these problems. Write the times as they would appear on a digital clock.

Brianna left for her violin class at 2:45 PM. It took her 15 minutes to get there. After a one-hour lesson, it took her 15 minutes to walk home. What time did she arrive home?

School begins at 8:15 AM. It takes Alison about 10 minutes to walk to school. Her friend Usha needs about 20 minutes to get to school.

What time should Alison leave to be on time?

What time should Usha leave to be on time?

Morgan and Taylor spent the morning skating. They stopped for lunch for half an hour at 1:00 PM, and then skated for another 30 minutes. What time did they finish skating?

Fiona left school at 3:15 PM. It took her 20 minutes to walk to the library. She worked there for an hour and then went home. What time did she leave the library?

Aziz had two exams today. The first one started at 8:30 AM and ended 45 minutes later. What time did it end?

His second exam began at 10:15 AM and ended at 10:45 AM. How long did the second exam last?

minutes

★ More Time Problems

GOAL

Learn to use a schedule.

To Midtown Stadium		
From Greenport	**Franklin**	**Midtown Stadium**
9:15 AM	10:35 AM	11:50 AM
10:15 AM	11:35 AM	12:50 PM
11:15 AM	12:35 AM	1:50 PM
To Greenport		
From Midtown Stadium	**Franklin**	**Greenport**
3:00 PM	4:15 PM	4:25 PM
4:00 PM	5:15 PM	6:25 PM
5:00 PM	6:15 PM	7:25 PM

Jenny and Fran are going to watch a tennis match tomorrow at the Midtown Stadium. Use the train schedule above to answer these problems.

The match begins at 12:15 PM. What time should Jenny take the train from Greenport to get to the stadium on time?

Fran plans to get on the same train at Franklin. What time is that train expected to reach Franklin?

After the match, Jenny and Fran leave the stadium at 4:30 PM. What time is the next train back to Greenport?

What time will Fran get off the train at Franklin?

What time will Jenny get off the train at Greenport?

$ × ÷ % = $ + ? — × ÷ % = $? + — % × ÷ = $ + ? — × ÷ %

More Time Problems

> Learn to read timelines. A timeline is a way of displaying events in the order in which they occurred, or in which you plan to do them.

Look at the timeline below that Carlo and Elda made to plan their work on a science project.

Monday	**Wednesday**	**Friday**
Look up information	Write report	Present project

Tuesday	**Thursday**
Search for pictures	Practice presenting project

Now use the information on the timeline to complete these sentences.

On Wednesday, they will write their ....

On Monday, they will look up .... to write their report.

On Thursday, they will practice .... their project.

On Tuesday, they will search for .... to illustrate their report.

On Friday, they will present their .... at the science fair.

Alice and her dad went to the Evergreen Harvest Festival.
Here are some of the things they did there.
At 10:00 AM, Alice won a doll at a carnival game.
At 11:00 AM, Alice had her face painted to look like a cat.
At 12:00 PM, Alice and her dad ate cheese sandwiches for lunch.
Finally, at 1:00 PM, Alice and her dad bought a brownie to share.

Now write these events on the timeline below.

10:00 AM		12:00 PM	
	11:00 AM		1:00 PM

$\times \div \% = \$ + ? - \times \div \% = \$? + - \% \times \div = \$ + ? - \times \div \%$

★ Pie Charts

Learn to read pie charts. A pie chart is a circular graph divided into sections. The size of each section represents the data for each category.

Students in Ms. Berry's class all love pies. This pie chart shows the kinds of pies they like best.

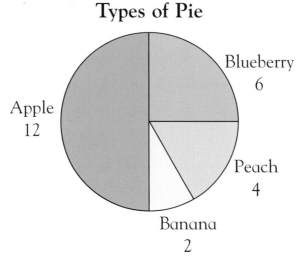

Types of Pie

Blueberry 6

Apple 12

Peach 4

Banana 2

Now use the information on the pie chart to answer these questions.

How many children are there in Ms. Berry's class? ⬚ children

How many children in Ms. Berry's class like peach pies best? ⬚ children

How many more children like apple pie best than like peach pie best? ⬚ children

Which pie did most of the children say they liked best? ....

Which pie did the fewest number of children like best? ....

Which two pies did a total of ten children like best? ....

$\$\times\div\%=\$+?-\times\div\%=\$?+-\%\times\div=\$+?-\times\div\%$

Learn to collect information from a line graph.

Lana and Max tracked the changes in the price of a gallon of milk every year for six years. They made this line graph to show the data that they collected.

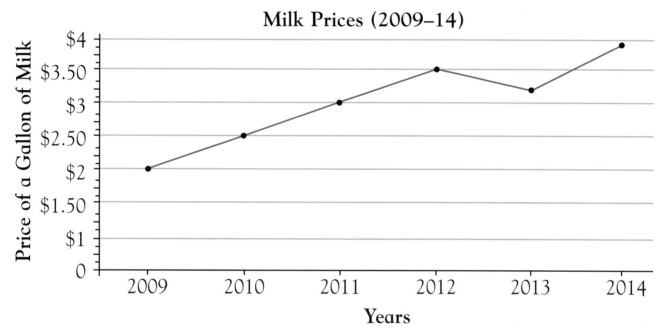

Milk Prices (2009–14)

Now use the information on the graph to answer these questions. Circle the correct answers.

In which year was the price of a gallon of milk at its highest?

2011   2013   2014

Which is the only year when the price was lower than the previous year?

2010   2011   2013

What was the lowest price for a gallon milk in the time period shown?

$2.50 $2 $3.25

How much more did a gallon of milk cost in 2012 than it did in 2009?

$1.25   50¢ $1.50

★ Bar Graphs

Learn to collect information from a horizontal bar graph.

The horizontal bar graph below shows the duration of different rides in an amusement park.

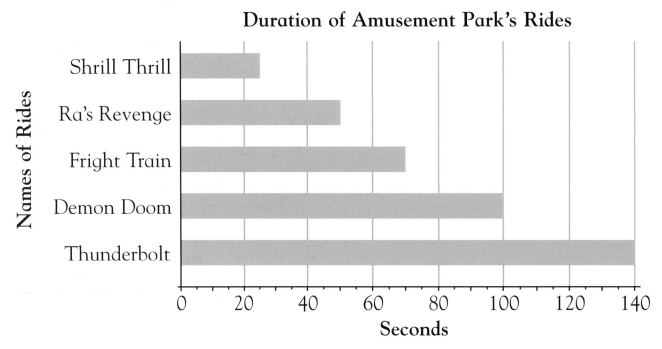

Duration of Amusement Park's Rides

Now use the information shown on the graph to answer these questions.

Which ride is the longest? ....

Which ride will take half as long as the Thunderbolt? ....

Which ride will be over in less than half a minute? ....

Which ride lasts twice as long as the Shrill Thrill? ....

Which ride will last for 100 seconds? ....

Which ride will last more than two minutes? ....

$ × ÷ % = $ + ? − × ÷ % = $? + − % × ÷ = $ + ? − × ÷ %

GOAL

Learn to collect information from a vertical bar graph.

The vertical bar graph below shows the heights of some of the tallest buildings in the United States.

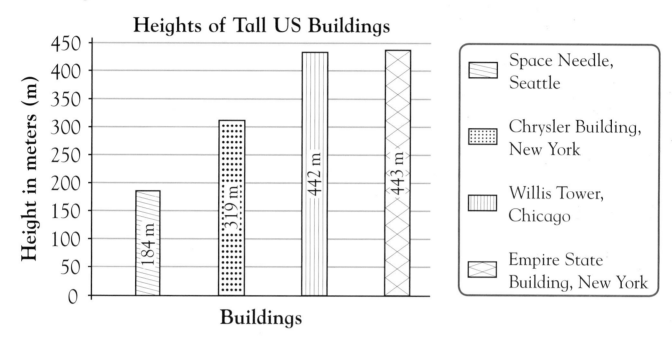

Now use the information shown on the graph to answer these questions.

Which building shown on the graph is the shortest?

....

Which building is a meter shorter than the tallest building?

....

Which building's height in meters is an odd number with 1 in the tens place?

....

Which building is 124 m taller than the Chrysler Building?

....

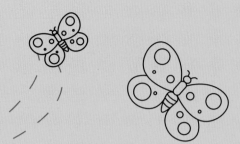

Certificate

3rd Grade

Congratulations to

....

for successfully finishing this book.

GOOD JOB!

You're a star.

⭐ ⭐ ⭐ ⭐ ⭐

Date

Answer Section with Parents' Notes

This book is intended to teach math problem solving to third grade children. The content is designed to feature problems similar to those they may encounter in everyday life.

Contents
By working through this book, your child will practice:
- identifying place value in four-digit numbers;
- two-step word problems involving addition and subtraction;
- using the multiplication facts from 2 through 12 to solve problems;
- finding missing factors of multiplication to solve problems;
- division with remainders;
- solving word problems related to money and time;
- solving measurement problems using Imperial and metric units;
- identifying 2-dimensional and 3-dimensional shapes;
- representing fractions on number lines;
- adding and subtracting fractions;
- interpreting and showing data on bar graphs, pie graphs, and line graphs.

How to Help Your Child
Guide your child by reading the problems and instructions slowly. Make sure he or she understands the questions, the concepts involved, and the different math terms being used.

As you work with your child, you will get an idea of what he or she finds easy, as well as what is more challenging. Use a hands-on approach to help your child understand any concepts he or she finds difficult to grasp. For example, use blocks or other objects found around the home to practice counting, adding, and multiplying. It may also be useful to have a small chalkboard to jot down numbers and to draw on.

Remember to build your child's confidence by praising success. Encourage your child to persist when faced with small challenges. Always remember that finding solutions to math problems should be exciting.

★ Place Value

Learn about place value in numbers with up to four digits.

Write the place value of the underlined digit in each number.

6,<u>3</u>76   Hundreds   <u>4</u>,201   Thousands

8,2<u>8</u>9   Tens   2,25<u>4</u>   Ones

Write these numbers as numerals.

Five thousand two hundred three	5,203
One thousand one hundred thirty-two	1,132
Six hundred two	602
Four thousand two hundred twenty-six	4,226
Seven hundred five	705

Write these numerals as number words.

565	Five hundred sixty-five
908	Nine hundred eight
3,457	Three thousand four hundred fifty-seven
9,389	Nine thousand three hundred eighty-nine
7,691	Seven thousand six hundred ninety-one

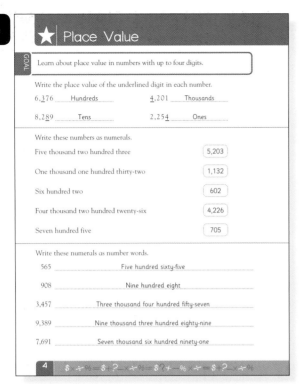

Help your child study the concept of place value. Encourage him or her to draw vertical lines between the place values, especially when adding or subtracting numbers with three or more digits. To draw attention to place values, read aloud larger numbers.

Place Value ★

Practice identifying place value.

Last summer, the baseball teams from every school in the Sun City district got together and played against each other. The scores are shown on the chart below.

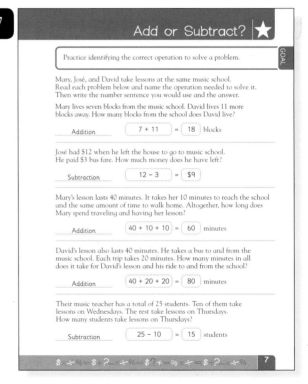

Teams	Score (Number of Hits)
Sun City East	14
Sun City North	7
Sun City West	3
Sun City South	11

How many hits did the school teams score altogether?   35

In this number, what digit is in the ones place?   5

How many hits did Sun City East and Sun City West score altogether? Write the answer.

17

In this number, what digit is in the

ones place?   7

tens place?   1

Multiply the total number of hits scored by 10. Write the answer.

350

In this number, what digit is in the

ones place?   0

tens place?   5

hundreds place?   3

A data problem with multiple questions like the one on this page may seem slightly overwhelming at first. It is important for your child to follow and organize the facts provided. Explain to him or her that taking notes or circling facts as he or she reads through the problem may be helpful.

★ Add or Subtract?

Learn to identify the operation needed to solve a problem.

Jaiden and his family have recently moved to San Francisco. Read each problem below. First name the operation needed to solve it. Then write the number sentence you would use and the answer.

Today, the temperature in San Francisco is 64°F. The weather forecast for tomorrow predicts it will be 11°F warmer. What will the temperature be tomorrow?

Addition   64°F + 11°F = 75°F

Jaiden and his sister Natalie walk to school, which is only four blocks away. Their neighbor Paul takes a bus to his school, which is 20 blocks away. How many more blocks than Jaiden and Natalie does Paul travel to school?

Subtraction   20 – 4 = 16 blocks

Jaiden and Natalie go for a swim. The water temperature of the pool is 83°F. It has gone up 10°F since yesterday. What was the temperature yesterday?

Subtraction   83°F – 10°F = 73°F

Mom wants to plant basil and tomatoes in the garden. She has space for 40 rows of plants. She plants 12 rows of basil. How many rows of tomatoes can she plant?

Subtraction   40 – 12 = 28 rows

Dad, however, wants to plant ten rows of corn, seven rows of parsley, and three rows of mint. How many rows is this altogether?

Addition   10 + 7 + 3 = 20 rows

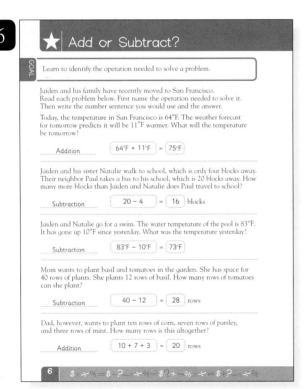

As your child reads a word problem, he or she must learn to recognize what information is needed to solve the problem, and what is not. Check your child's understanding by asking which pieces of information in the problem are important.

Add or Subtract? ★

Practice identifying the correct operation to solve a problem.

Mary, José, and David take lessons at the same music school. Read each problem below and name the operation needed to solve it. Then write the number sentence you would use and the answer.

Mary lives seven blocks from the music school. David lives 11 more blocks away. How many blocks from the school does David live?

Addition   7 + 11 = 18 blocks

José had $12 when he left the house to go to music school. He paid $3 bus fare. How much money does he have left?

Subtraction   12 – 3 = $9

Mary's lesson lasts 40 minutes. It takes her 10 minutes to reach the school and the same amount of time to walk home. Altogether, how long does Mary spend traveling and having her lesson?

Addition   40 + 10 + 10 = 60 minutes

David's lesson also lasts 40 minutes. He takes a bus to and from the music school. Each trip takes 20 minutes. How many minutes in all does it take for David's lesson and his ride to and from the school?

Addition   40 + 20 + 20 = 80 minutes

Their music teacher has a total of 25 students. Ten of them take lessons on Wednesdays. The rest take lessons on Thursdays. How many students take lessons on Thursdays?

Subtraction   25 – 10 = 15 students

Be sure to adopt a "math is fun" attitude with your child. Avoid giving your child the message that math is difficult or complex. Point out the use of numbers and math in daily life.

★ More Addition & Subtraction

GOAL Learn to solve problems using multiple operations.

Ava went to the movies with her dad. Read each of the problems below. Then figure out the answers, writing out the number sentences you use in the boxes given below. **Hint:** Each problem has two steps.

Ava counted 157 people in the theater at the start of the movie. Ten people came in after it started. At intermission, Ava saw 12 people leave. How many people remained in the theater?

155 people

$157 + 10 = 167$
$167 - 12 = 155$

Ava waited in line to buy popcorn. There were four people ahead of her and five behind her. How many people in all were waiting in line? If each person took two minutes to buy popcorn, how long did Ava have to wait for her turn?

10 people
8 minutes

$4 + 1 + 5 = 10$
$2 + 2 + 2 + 2 = 8$

The popcorn made Ava thirsty. Her dad gave her $5 to buy two bottles of water. One bottle cost $2. How much did Ava pay for two bottles? How much change did she receive?

$\$4$
$\$1$

$2 + 2 = 4$
$5 - 4 = 1$

Ava then saw a pack of her favorite cookies. They cost $8. If Ava had two dollars, how much more money would she need to buy the cookies? If she bought fruit chews for a dollar instead, how much change should she expect?

$\$6$
$\$1$

$8 - 2 = 6$
$2 - 1 = 1$

Try writing some extra addition and subtraction problems for your child to solve. Keep them simple, but engaging. Solve the first few with your child, and then let him or her complete the rest independently. Assess your child's work, as needed, to see how well he or she is doing.

More Addition & Subtraction ★

GOAL Practice solving addition and subtraction problems.

Figure out the answers to these problems.

In Brandon's school, there are 137 girls and 250 boys altogether in 2nd and 3rd grade. There are also 100 girls and 104 boys in 4th grade. How many children in 2nd, 3rd, and 4th grades attend Brandon's school?

591 children

A bus driver picks up 13 people at the first stop, 22 people at the second stop, and 23 people at the third stop. How many passengers are now on the bus?

58 passengers

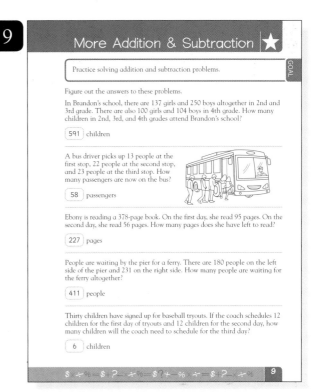

Ebony is reading a 378-page book. On the first day, she read 95 pages. On the second day, she read 56 pages. How many pages does she have left to read?

227 pages

People are waiting by the pier for a ferry. There are 180 people on the left side of the pier and 231 on the right side. How many people are waiting for the ferry altogether?

411 people

Thirty children have signed up for baseball tryouts. If the coach schedules 12 children for the first day of tryouts and 12 children for the second day, how many children will the coach need to schedule for the third day?

6 children

As your child solves problems that involve multiple calculations, help him or her to see that the same problem can be solved in different ways. For example, to solve problems 4 and 5 on this page, he or she can subtract each number from the total or add the numbers and then subtract.

★ Multiply by 2 & 3

GOAL Learn to solve problems using the 2x and 3x tables.

Figure out the answers to these problems.

Leo has twice as many blue shirts as red shirts. If Leo has three red shirts, how many blue shirts does he have?

6 blue shirts

Leo's puppy Skippy eats two cans of food a day. How many cans of food does Skippy eat in a week?

14 cans

There are ten tables in Leo's classroom. Each table has two activities on it. How many activities are there altogether in the classroom?

20 activities

Figure out the answers to these problems.

A pair of socks costs $3. Maria wants three pairs. How much money does she need to buy them?

$\$9$

Maria decides to bake cookies for three of her friends. She wants to give four cookies to each of them. How many cookies does she need to bake?

12 cookies

Maria spends three days a week on a school project. It takes her five weeks to complete it. How many days does Maria spend on the project altogether?

15 days

Make sure your child knows that the equations used to solve these problems can be written either horizontally or vertically. Encourage your child to solve problems without being afraid of making mistakes. Making mistakes is a part of learning!

Multiply by 4 & 5 ★

GOAL Learn to solve problems using the 4x and 5x tables.

Figure out the answers to these problems.

Scarlet is learning to play the violin. She has four lessons a month. How many lessons does she have in a year?

48 lessons

Scarlet and four of her friends sell tickets for a school concert. They sell four tickets each. How many tickets do they sell between them?

20 tickets

Scarlet plays her violin at the concert. She and the other musicians sit in four rows on the stage. There are eight musicians in each row. How many musicians are there altogether?

32 members

Figure out the answers to these problems.

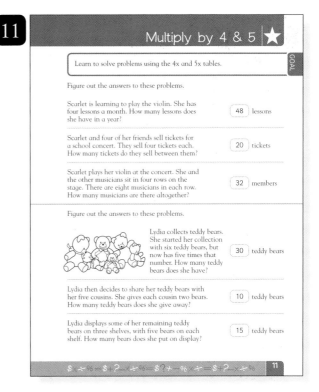

Lydia collects teddy bears. She started her collection with six teddy bears, but now has five times that number. How many teddy bears does she have?

30 teddy bears

Lydia then decides to share her teddy bears with her five cousins. She gives each cousin two bears. How many teddy bears does she give away?

10 teddy bears

Lydia displays some of her remaining teddy bears on three shelves, with five bears on each shelf. How many bears does she put on display?

15 teddy bears

Make sure that your child understands that multiplying means adding the same number together several times. Whenever necessary, review times tables with your child. Chanting them repeatedly to a rhythm helps children memorize them.

★ Factors

Multiply by 6 ★

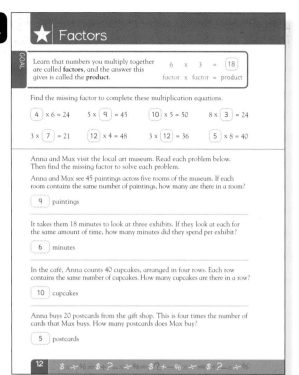

GOAL: Learn that numbers you multiply together are called **factors**, and the answer this gives is called the **product**.

$6 \times 3 = 18$

factor × factor = product

Find the missing factor to complete these multiplication equations.

$4 \times 6 = 24$ $5 \times 9 = 45$ $10 \times 5 = 50$ $8 \times 3 = 24$

$3 \times 7 = 21$ $12 \times 4 = 48$ $3 \times 12 = 36$ $5 \times 8 = 40$

Anna and Max visit the local art museum. Read each problem below. Then find the missing factor to solve each problem.

Anna and Max see 45 paintings across five rooms of the museum. If each room contains the same number of paintings, how many are there in a room?

9 paintings

It takes them 18 minutes to look at three exhibits. If they look at each for the same amount of time, how many minutes did they spend per exhibit?

6 minutes

In the café, Anna counts 40 cupcakes, arranged in four rows. Each row contains the same number of cupcakes. How many cupcakes are there in a row?

10 cupcakes

Anna buys 20 postcards from the gift shop. This is four times the number of cards that Max buys. How many postcards does Max buy?

5 postcards

Solving problems with missing factors can help your child recall multiplication facts, and give your child a solid base for division problems. For example, if your child knows 4 x 6 = 24, they can better understand that 24 ÷ 6 = 4.

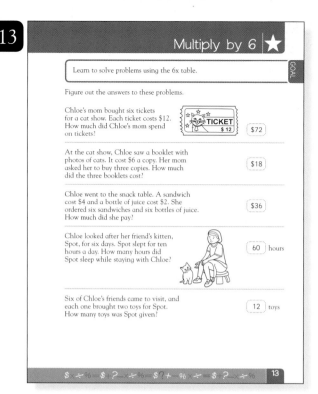

GOAL: Learn to solve problems using the 6x table.

Figure out the answers to these problems.

Chloe's mom bought six tickets for a cat show. Each ticket costs $12. How much did Chloe's mom spend on tickets?

$72

At the cat show, Chloe saw a booklet with photos of cats. It cost $6 a copy. Her mom asked her to buy three copies. How much did the three booklets cost?

$18

Chloe went to the snack table. A sandwich cost $4 and a bottle of juice cost $2. She ordered six sandwiches and six bottles of juice. How much did she pay?

$36

Chloe looked after her friend's kitten, Spot, for six days. Spot slept for ten hours a day. How many hours did Spot sleep while staying with Chloe?

60 hours

Six of Chloe's friends came to visit, and each one brought two toys for Spot. How many toys was Spot given?

12 toys

If necessary, suggest to your child ways to recall multiplication facts. For example, if your child cannot recall a multiplication fact, such as 6 x 3, as him or her to think of what 6 x 2 + 6 is or 6 + 6 + 6 is. The answer is 18!

14

★ Multiply by 7

Multiply by 8 ★

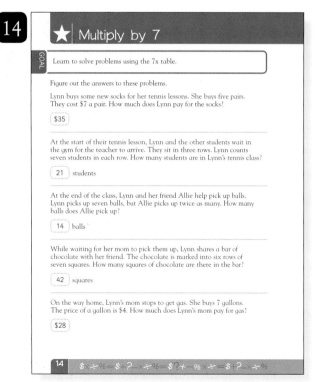

GOAL: Learn to solve problems using the 7x table.

Figure out the answers to these problems.

Lynn buys new socks for her tennis lessons. She buys five pairs. They cost $7 a pair. How much does Lynn pay for the socks?

$35

At the start of their tennis lesson, Lynn and the other students wait in the gym for the teacher to arrive. They sit in three rows. Lynn counts seven students in each row. How many students are in Lynn's tennis class?

21 students

At the end of the class, Lynn and her friend Allie help pick up balls. Lynn picks up seven balls, but Allie picks up twice as many. How many balls does Allie pick up?

14 balls

While waiting for her mom to pick them up, Lynn shares a bar of chocolate with her friend. The chocolate is marked into six rows of seven squares. How many squares of chocolate are there in the bar?

42 squares

On the way home, Lynn's mom stops to get gas. She buys 7 gallons. The price of a gallon is $4. How much does Lynn's mom pay for gas?

$28

As the number you multiply by increases, some children find recalling facts for times tables particularly challenging. It may be useful to run through the 7x table with your child before trying to solve the problems on this page.

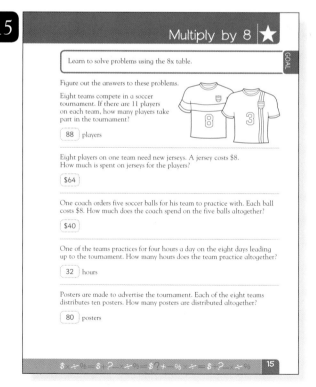

GOAL: Learn to solve problems using the 8x table.

Figure out the answers to these problems.

Eight teams compete in a soccer tournament. If there are 11 players on each team, how many players take part in the tournament?

88 players

Eight players on one team need new jerseys. A jersey costs $8. How much is spent on jerseys for the players?

$64

One coach orders five soccer balls for his team to practice with. Each ball costs $8. How much does the coach spend on the five balls altogether?

$40

One of the teams practices for four hours a day on the eight days leading up to the tournament. How many hours does the team practice altogether?

32 hours

Posters are made to advertise the tournament. Each of the eight teams distributes ten posters. How many posters are distributed altogether?

80 posters

Keep reviewing times tables with your child. Remember that committing times tables to memory gives your child automatic recall of the facts, saving time when solving multiplication problems.

★ Multiply by 9

Learn to solve problems using the 9x table.

Figure out the answers to these problems.

Jean is preparing dinner for nine people. She plans to serve them two fish cakes each. How many fish cakes must she make?

18 fish cakes

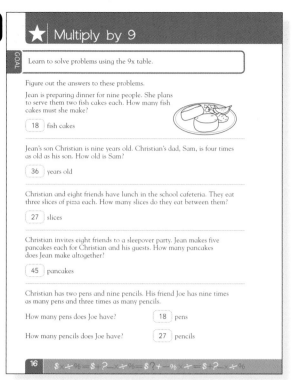

Jean's son Christian is nine years old. Christian's dad, Sam, is four times as old as his son. How old is Sam?

36 years old

Christian and eight friends have lunch in the school cafeteria. They eat three slices of pizza each. How many slices do they eat between them?

27 slices

Christian invites eight friends to a sleepover party. Jean makes five pancakes each for Christian and his guests. How many pancakes does Jean make altogether?

45 pancakes

Christian has two pens and nine pencils. His friend Joe has nine times as many pens and three times as many pencils.

How many pens does Joe have? **18** pens

How many pencils does Joe have? **27** pencils

If your child has problems multiplying a number by 9, ask him or her to try this strategy. First multiply the number by 10, for example, 7 x 10, which equals 70. Then explain that to find the product of 7 x 9, you subtract 7 from 70 and arrive at the answer, which is 63.

Multiply by 10 ★

Learn to solve problems using the 10x table.

Figure out the answers to these problems.

Ethan collects baseball cards and wants to buy ten more from his friend Jim. Jim asks $2 for each card. How much must Ethan pay Jim for the ten cards?

$20

Jim has been collecting baseball cards for four years. In that time, his dad has given him ten rare cards every year as a birthday gift. How many rare cards has Jim's dad given him so far?

40 cards

For Christmas, Jim receives three more cards from his dad. Ethan is also given some baseball cards for Christmas, but he receives ten times as many as Jim. How many cards does Ethan get for Christmas?

30 cards

In January, Jim and Ethan challenge each other to see who can collect the most cards that month. Ethan collects five cards, but Jim collects ten times that number. How many baseball cards does Jim collect in January?

50 cards

Lee and Jake also collect baseball cards. Lee has collected ten new cards a month for two years. Jake has collected ten cards a month, but only for one year. How many baseball cards do they have altogether?

360 cards

The 10x table is one of the easiest to learn. Make sure your child knows that multiplying a number by 10 involves simply writing a zero after the number. For example, 2 x 10 = 20, 5 x 10 = 50, and 8 x 10 = 80.

★ Multiply by 11

Learn to solve problems using the 11x table.

Figure out the answers to these problems.

Grace plays the piano. She has 11 days to prepare for a concert. She plans to practice for three hours a day. How many hours will she practice altogether?

33 hours

As well as playing on her own, Grace will also play two duets with a violinist. Each duet is 11 minutes long. How long will Grace and the violinist play together?

22 minutes

Grace buys a small gift for each of the eleven other musicians involved in the concert. Each gift costs $5. How much does Grace spend on the gifts?

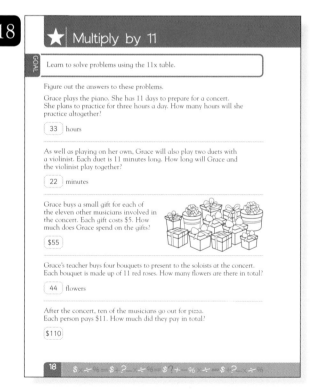

$55

Grace's teacher buys four bouquets to present to the soloists at the concert. Each bouquet is made up of 11 red roses. How many flowers are there in total?

44 flowers

After the concert, ten of the musicians go out for pizza. Each person pays $11. How much did they pay in total?

$110

Point out to your child that when multiplying any number up to 9 by 11, the product is the original number repeated. For example, 6 x 11 = 66 and 9 x 11 = 99. He or she should easily be able to determine that 10 x 11 = 110. Advise him or her to memorize 11 x 11 = 121 and 11 x 12 = 132.

Multiply by 12 ★

Learn to solve problems using the 12x table.
Remember: A dozen is another way of saying 12.

Figure out the answers to these problems.

Henry lives on a farm. On Monday, he collects a dozen eggs from the hen house. He collects twice that number on Tuesday. How many eggs does he collect on Tuesday? **24** eggs

Henry and his friends work six hours a day for 12 days to build a new chicken coop. How many hours in all does it take to finish the chicken coop? **72** hours

Henry's dog Summer has five puppies. He buys 12 bags of treats for each puppy. How many bags of treats does he buy? **60** bags

Henry's mom bakes four loaves of bread. She cuts each loaf into 12 slices. How many slices of bread does she have? **48** slices

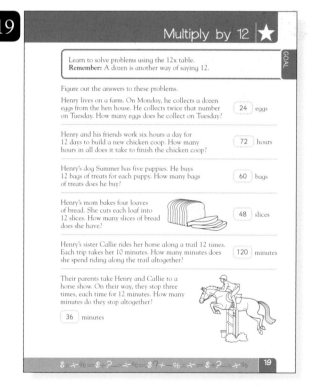

Henry's sister Callie rides her horse along a trail 12 times. Each trip takes her 10 minutes. How many minutes does she spend riding along the trail altogether? **120** minutes

Their parents take Henry and Callie to a horse show. On their way, they stop three times, each time for 12 minutes. How many minutes do they stop altogether?

36 minutes

If necessary, show your child an easy way of multiplying by larger numbers, such as 12. Split the large number up, multiply by the resulting parts, and then add the answers together. For example, 4 x 12 = (4 x 6) + (4 x 6) = 48.

★ More Multiplication

GOAL | Practice solving problems involving multiplication.

Figure out the answers to these problems.

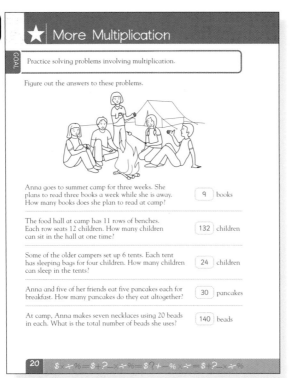

Anna goes to summer camp for three weeks. She plans to read three books a week while she is away. How many books does she plan to read at camp? **9** books

The food hall at camp has 11 rows of benches. Each row seats 12 children. How many children can sit in the hall at one time? **132** children

Some of the older campers set up 6 tents. Each tent has sleeping bags for four children. How many children can sleep in the tents? **24** children

Anna and five of her friends eat five pancakes each for breakfast. How many pancakes do they eat altogether? **30** pancakes

At camp, Anna makes seven necklaces using 20 beads in each. What is the total number of beads she uses? **140** beads

The problems on this page will help reinforce your child's skill at solving multiplication problems. Run through the 2x to 12x tables with your child before starting.

Properties of Multiplication ★

Learn three key properties of multiplication.

Commutative Property: The product of two numbers is the same regardless of the order of the factors. $7 \times 6 = 6 \times 7 = 42$

Associative Property: When you multiply three or more numbers, the product is the same regardless of how the factors are grouped. $(2 \times 6) \times 2 = 2 \times (6 \times 2) = 24$

Distributive Property: The sum of two numbers multiplied by a third number is equal to each addend times the third number. $4 \times 12 = 4 \times (10 + 2) = (4 \times 10) + (4 \times 2) = 48$

Solve the problems below. Then identify which property of multiplication you have used. Write **C** for "commutative property," **A** for "associative property," and **D** for "distributive property."

$(3 \times 6) \times 2 = 3 \times (6 \times 2) =$ **36** **A**

$8 \times 7 = 7 \times 8 =$ **56** **C**

$6 \times 12 = 6 \times (10 + 2) = (6 \times 10) + (6 \times 2) =$ **72** **D**

$9 \times 12 = 12 \times 9 =$ **108** **C**

$(9 \times 3) \times 2 = 9 \times (3 \times 2) =$ **54** **A**

$9 \times 7 = 9 \times (5 + 2) = (9 \times 5) + (9 \times 2) =$ **63** **D**

Many children may find it difficult to understand the definitions of the properties, so work carefully through the examples. You may also have to explain the use of parentheses in math equations.

★ Division

GOAL | Learn to divide. The number you are dividing is called the **dividend**. The number you divide by is called the **divisor**. The answer is called the **quotient**. Dividend → $6 ÷ 2 =$ **3** ← Quotient, Divisor

Remember: You can show division in different ways. For example: $12 ÷ 4$ is the same as $4\overline{)12}$ with 3 on top.

Answer each division problem. Then divide the objects shown into sets by circling them to match your answer. The first one has been done for you.

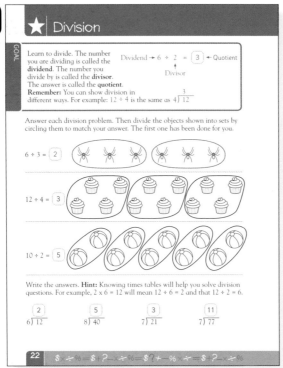

$6 ÷ 3 =$ **2**

$12 ÷ 4 =$ **3**

$10 ÷ 2 =$ **5**

Write the answers. **Hint:** Knowing times tables will help you solve division questions. For example, $2 \times 6 = 12$ will mean $12 ÷ 6 = 2$ and that $12 ÷ 2 = 6$.

$6\overline{)12}$ **2** $8\overline{)40}$ **5** $7\overline{)21}$ **3** $7\overline{)77}$ **11**

Use concrete objects, such as toothpicks, coins, and crayons, to explain division. Let your child see, touch, and divide the objects into groups. Write simple division problems, and let your child group objects to solve them. Regular reviewing of times tables, chanting them rhythmically, will help your child commit the facts to memory.

Division ★

GOAL | Practice division skills.

Write the answers.

$24 ÷ 4 =$ **6** $16 ÷ 4 =$ **4** $36 ÷ 6 =$ **6**

$48 ÷ 4 =$ **12** $72 ÷ 6 =$ **12** $56 ÷ 7 =$ **8**

$42 ÷ 7 =$ **6** $63 ÷ 7 =$ **9** $36 ÷ 12 =$ **3**

$80 ÷ 10 =$ **8** $120 ÷ 12 =$ **10** $100 ÷ 10 =$ **10**

Write the answers.

$2\overline{)12}$ **6** $5\overline{)20}$ **4** $7\overline{)49}$ **7** $8\overline{)24}$ **3**

$9\overline{)90}$ **10** $8\overline{)48}$ **6** $8\overline{)72}$ **9** $11\overline{)88}$ **8**

Point out the relationship of multiplication to division by demonstrating that the answer to a division equation (the quotient) can be checked by multiplying it by the divisor. The answer should be the same as the dividend. For example, $8 ÷ 4 = 2$ and $2 \times 4 = 8$.

★ Division Problems

GOAL Learn to solve problems using division.

Figure out the answers to these problems.

Lily and Catherine picked 30 apples. They divided them equally into three baskets. How many apples were in each basket?

[10] apples

Annie ordered a pizza for her three children. She cut the pizza into eight slices. The children were each given the same number of slices. How many slices did each child receive?

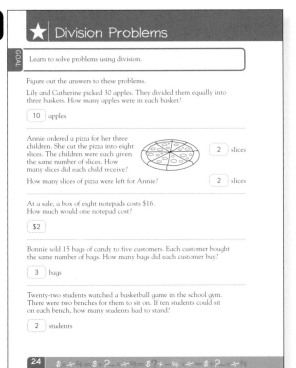

[2] slices

How many slices of pizza were left for Annie?

[2] slices

At a sale, a box of eight notepads costs $16. How much would one notepad cost?

[$2]

Bonnie sold 15 bags of candy to five customers. Each customer bought the same number of bags. How many bags did each customer buy?

[3] bags

Twenty-two students watched a basketball game in the school gym. There were two benches for them to sit on. If ten students could sit on each bench, how many students had to stand?

[2] students

This page introduces remainders, which may be a new concept for your child. Explain that when, after solving a division problem, there is a number left over, that number is called the remainder. For example, in the last problem on the page, the remaining number of students (2) had to stand, because there was no room left on the benches.

Division Problems ★

GOAL Practice solving problems using division.

Students from Parkside High School went out for lunch at the Brew Star Café. Read the menu below. Then figure out the answers to the problems under it. Show the number sentence you use in the box.

Brew Star Café Menu

Hot Dog .... $6   Pizza $5
Meatball Sub .... $7   All Drinks $2

Ella bought one drink each for her students. She paid $22. How many students did she buy drinks for?

[11] students   [22 ÷ 2 = 11]

Six students ordered the same item from the menu. Their bill came to $36. What did the students order? What was the price of that item?

They ordered hot dogs.   [$6]   [36 ÷ 6 = 6]

Sal placed an order for eight students, who all wanted the same item. The bill came to $56. What did Sal order? What did each one cost?

Sal ordered meatball subs.   [$7]   [56 ÷ 8 = 7]

At Nancy's table, three students ordered hot dogs and three ordered pizza. What was the total cost?

[$33]   [(3 × 6) + (3 × 5) = 33]

After your child has completed the activities on this page, review any questions he or she may have about division. Make sure he or she is clear about the meaning of terms such as dividend, divisor, and quotient, and understands the relationship between division and multiplication.

★ Math Terms

GOAL Study some common math terms.

s	u	b	t	r	a	c	t	p	d
x	f	j	h	z	f	d	g	r	i
r	a	v	j	z	k	u	s	o	v
u	c	v	m	j	q	j	d	i	i
g	t	v	e	h	k	t	u	d	d
j	o	u	c	r	f	r	s	c	e
k	r	h	x	o	s	o	k	t	n
r	s	p	d	l	u	d	n	r	d
s	e	f	t	i	n	e	d	r	c
q	u	o	t	i	e	n	t	e	e

In the word search puzzle, find and circle the math terms that match each description below. Then write each term next to its description.

To find the difference in value between two numbers.   Subtract

Numbers that are multiplied together.   Factors

Another name for the answer when multiplying.   Product

The product of any number multiplied by 0.   Zero

A number that is being divided.   Dividend

Another name for the answer when dividing.   Quotient

The word puzzle should help reinforce math terms and their meaning. Encourage your child to use the correct math terms as much as possible when talking about any issues they may have with solving problems.

Mixed Problems ★

GOAL Practice finding the correct operation to solve a problem.

Read each problem below and name the operation needed to solve it. Then figure out the answer.

Ted has $42 and Sue has $19. They want to buy a video game to share, which costs $60. Do they have enough money to buy the game?

Addition   Yes

Annette weighs 75 pounds. Her friend Jane weighs 10 pounds less. What does Jane weigh?

Subtraction   [65] pounds

Finley is waiting on line to buy tickets to the zoo. He counts 13 people ahead of him. If each person takes about two minutes to buy tickets, how long will Finley have to wait on line?

Multiplication   [26] minutes

Noah and Danny gather acorns in the park. Noah picks up 44 acorns, but Danny only picks up half as many. How many acorns does Danny pick up?

Division   [22] acorns

Bella takes three of her friends out for ice-cream sundaes. Two girls can share one sundae. How many sundaes does Bella need to buy? A sundae costs $6. How much does Bella spend?

Division   [2] sundaes

Multiplication   [$12]

If necessary, identify the steps necessary for solving each part of a problem for your child. In time, he or she should be able to do this independently and will begin to enjoy solving math problems.

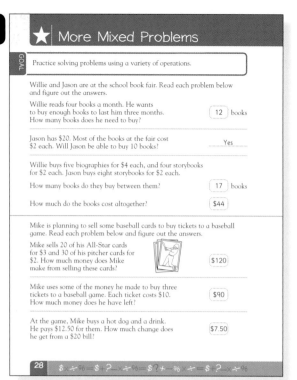

★ More Mixed Problems

GOAL Practice solving problems using a variety of operations.

Willie and Jason are at the school book fair. Read each problem below and figure out the answers.

Willie reads four books a month. He wants to buy enough books to last him three months. How many books does he need to buy?

[12] books

Jason has $20. Most of the books at the fair cost $2 each. Will Jason be able to buy 10 books?

Yes

Willie buys five biographies for $4 each, and four storybooks for $2 each. Jason buys eight storybooks for $2 each.

How many books do they buy between them?

[17] books

How much do the books cost altogether?

[$44]

Mike is planning to sell some baseball cards to buy tickets to a baseball game. Read each problem below and figure out the answers.

Mike sells 20 of his All-Star cards for $3 and 30 of his pitcher cards for $2. How much money does Mike make from selling these cards?

[$120]

Mike uses some of the money he made to buy three tickets to a baseball game. Each ticket costs $10. How much money does he have left?

[$90]

At the game, Mike buys a hot dog and a drink. He pays $12.50 for them. How much change does he get from a $20 bill?

[$7.50]

Remember that if your child is struggling with the problems on this page, it may be useful to go through them with him or her first, figuring out the operations needed to solve each one.

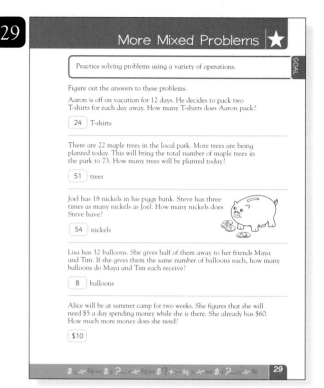

More Mixed Problems ★

GOAL Practice solving problems using a variety of operations.

Figure out the answers to these problems.

Aaron is off on vacation for 12 days. He decides to pack two T-shirts for each day away. How many T-shirts does Aaron pack?

[24] T-shirts

There are 22 maple trees in the local park. More trees are being planted today. This will bring the total number of maple trees in the park to 73. How many trees will be planted today?

[51] trees

Joel has 18 nickels in his piggy bank. Steve has three times as many nickels as Joel. How many nickels does Steve have?

[54] nickels

Lisa has 32 balloons. She gives half of them away to her friends Maya and Tim. If she gives them the same number of balloons each, how many balloons do Maya and Tim each receive?

[8] balloons

Alice will be at summer camp for two weeks. She figures that she will need $5 a day spending money while she is there. She already has $60. How much more money does she need?

[$10]

Solving problems involving a variety of operations, like the ones on this page, is a great way to sharpen your child's math skills. Your child should begin to understand more fully the relationship between numbers when adding, subtracting, multiplying, and dividing.

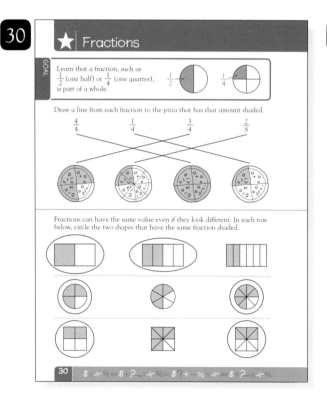

★ Fractions

GOAL Learn that a fraction, such as $\frac{1}{2}$ (one half) or $\frac{1}{4}$ (one quarter), is part of a whole.

$\frac{1}{2}$ $\frac{1}{4}$

Draw a line from each fraction to the pizza that has that amount shaded.

$\frac{4}{4}$ $\frac{1}{4}$ $\frac{3}{4}$ $\frac{2}{8}$

Fractions can have the same value even if they look different. In each row below, circle the two shapes that have the same fraction shaded.

Cut an apple or banana into four parts to show your child how the parts represent fractions of the whole fruit. Write different fractions on cards, and ask your child to match cards with fractions of the fruit. Point out that all the parts of the fruit represent a whole number ($\frac{4}{4}$ = 1).

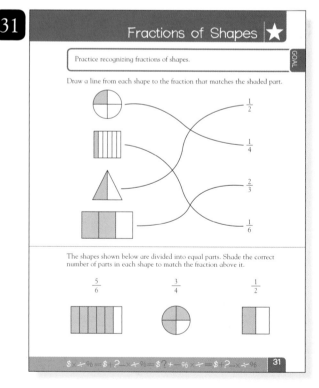

Fractions of Shapes ★

GOAL Practice recognizing fractions of shapes.

Draw a line from each shape to the fraction that matches the shaded part.

$\frac{1}{2}$

$\frac{1}{4}$

$\frac{2}{3}$

$\frac{1}{6}$

The shapes shown below are divided into equal parts. Shade the correct number of parts in each shape to match the fraction above it.

$\frac{5}{6}$ $\frac{3}{4}$ $\frac{1}{2}$

Give your child some graph paper and let him or her draw a variety of shapes on it with colored pencils. Divide each shape into equal sections, and then ask your child to shade them to match different fractions.

★ Fractions

Fractions ★

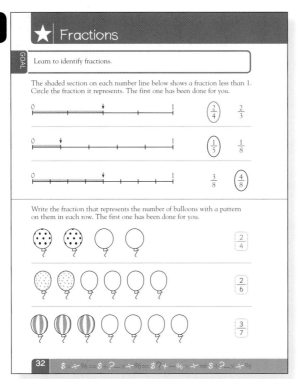

GOAL Learn to identify fractions.

The shaded section on each number line below shows a fraction less than 1. Circle the fraction it represents. The first one has been done for you.

$\frac{2}{4}$ $\frac{2}{3}$

$\frac{1}{5}$ $\frac{1}{8}$

$\frac{3}{8}$ $\frac{4}{8}$

Write the fraction that represents the number of balloons with a pattern on them in each row. The first one has been done for you.

$\frac{2}{4}$

$\frac{2}{6}$

$\frac{3}{7}$

A number line gives your child a visual and linear representation of the value of fractions. Explain that the fractions represented above are parts of 1. Also explain that fractions such as $\frac{3}{3}$ and $\frac{5}{5}$ equal 1, and that fractions such as $\frac{3}{2}$ and $\frac{8}{6}$ are greater than 1.

GOAL Practice identifying fractions.

Write the missing fractions in the boxes along these number lines.

0 $\frac{1}{10}$ $\frac{2}{10}$ $\frac{3}{10}$ $\frac{4}{10}$ $\frac{5}{10}$ $\frac{6}{10}$ $\frac{7}{10}$ $\frac{8}{10}$ $\frac{9}{10}$ 1

0 $\frac{1}{4}$ $\frac{2}{4}$ $\frac{3}{4}$ 1 $1\frac{1}{4}$ $1\frac{2}{4}$ $1\frac{3}{4}$ 2

0 $\frac{1}{6}$ $\frac{2}{6}$ $\frac{3}{6}$ $\frac{4}{6}$ $\frac{5}{6}$ 1 $1\frac{1}{6}$ $1\frac{2}{6}$ $1\frac{3}{6}$ $1\frac{4}{6}$ $1\frac{5}{6}$ 2

0 $\frac{1}{8}$ $\frac{2}{8}$ $\frac{3}{8}$ $\frac{4}{8}$ $\frac{5}{8}$ $\frac{6}{8}$ $\frac{7}{8}$ 1

Color in $\frac{2}{5}$ of these fish.

Color in $\frac{4}{8}$ of these rabbits.

Explain to your child that $\frac{1}{3}$ of a group of objects is just another way of saying 1 out of every 3 of those objects, and that $\frac{1}{2}$ of them is the same as 1 out of every 2. That will let your child grow accustomed to reading and hearing fractions expressed in different ways.

★ 2-D Shapes

3-D Shapes ★

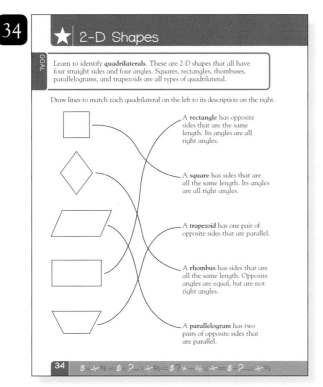

GOAL Learn to identify **quadrilaterals**. These are 2-D shapes that all have four straight sides and four angles. Squares, rectangles, rhombuses, parallelograms, and trapezoids are all types of quadrilateral.

Draw lines to match each quadrilateral on the left to its description on the right.

A **rectangle** has opposite sides that are the same length. Its angles are all right angles.

A **square** has sides that are all the same length. Its angles are all right angles.

A **trapezoid** has one pair of opposite sides that are parallel.

A **rhombus** has sides that are all the same length. Opposite angles are equal, but are not right angles.

A **parallelogram** has two pairs of opposite sides that are parallel.

Cut colored paper into several different quadrilaterals, and put them into a bag. With your child, take turns to pick shapes out of the bag and name them. Talk about how some are similar, while others are different.

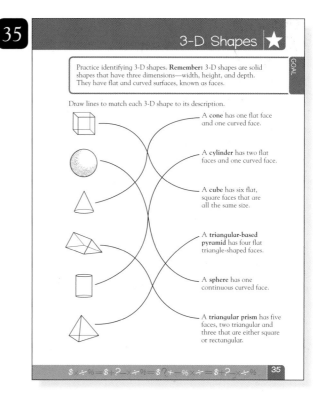

GOAL Practice identifying 3-D shapes. **Remember:** 3-D shapes are solid shapes that have three dimensions—width, height, and depth. They have flat and curved surfaces, known as faces.

Draw lines to match each 3-D shape to its description.

A **cone** has one flat face and one curved face.

A **cylinder** has two flat faces and one curved face.

A **cube** has six flat, square faces that are all the same size.

A **triangular-based pyramid** has four flat triangle-shaped faces.

A **sphere** has one continuous curved face.

A **triangular prism** has five faces, two triangular and three that are either square or rectangular.

Reinforce 2-D and 3-D shapes by showing your child the difference between a drawing of a flat square and that of a cube, and between the drawing of a circle and that of a sphere or a ball. Use the words "height," "width," "depth," and "faces" when describing 3-D shapes.

★ Measuring Length

GOAL Practice measuring length, using both inches and centimeters.

How long are these items? First use a ruler marked in inches to measure them. Then use a ruler marked in centimeters. **Note:** Remember to put either **in** (for inches) or **cm** (for centimeters) as part of your answer.

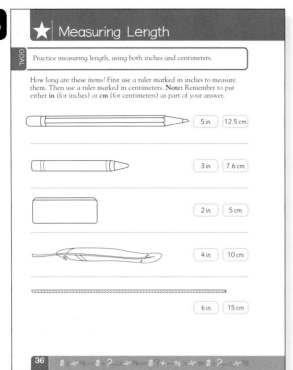

5 in   12.5 cm

3 in   7.6 cm

2 in   5 cm

4 in   10 cm

6 in   15 cm

Using tools, such as a ruler or tape measure, gives your child a frame of reference and a sense of authenticity when measuring objects. Remember that it is crucial that your child learns both the imperial and metric systems of measurement.

Perimeters ★

GOAL

Learn to calculate perimeters. **Note:** The perimeter of a shape is the distance around its outer edge. For example:

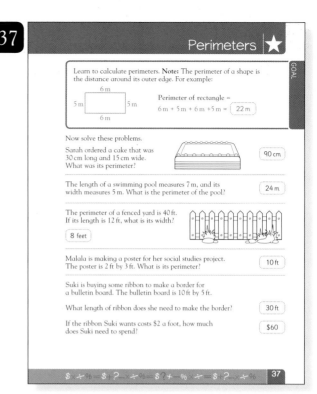

Perimeter of rectangle =
6 m + 5 m + 6 m + 5 m = 22 m

Now solve these problems.

Sarah ordered a cake that was 30 cm long and 15 cm wide. What was its perimeter?   90 cm

The length of a swimming pool measures 7 m, and its width measures 5 m. What is the perimeter of the pool?   24 m

The perimeter of a fenced yard is 40 ft. If its length is 12 ft, what is its width?   8 feet

Malala is making a poster for her social studies project. The poster is 2 ft by 3 ft. What is its perimeter?   10 ft

Suki is buying some ribbon to make a border for a bulletin board. The bulletin board is 10 ft by 5 ft.

What length of ribbon does she need to make the border?   30 ft

If the ribbon Suki wants costs $2 a foot, how much does Suki need to spend? $60

Reinforce real-world math problems by challenging your child to find the perimeters of various shapes and spaces. Provide him or her with the lengths and widths. Then provide the perimeter and the length of one side and ask for the length of the other side.

★ Measuring Area

GOAL Learn to measure the area of a 2-D shape. **Note:** The area of a shape is the amount of space it covers. You can measure area using squares. Each square is a square unit. For example:

Area of the rectangle = 24 square units
or (8 × 3) square units
or **length × width**

Figure out the answers to these problems.

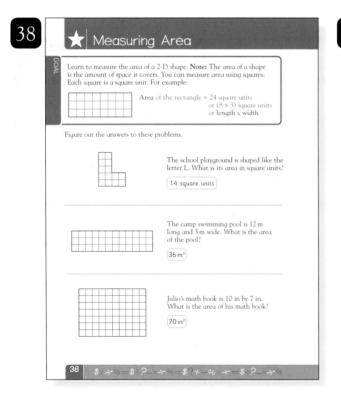

The school playground is shaped like the letter L. What is its area in square units?   14 square units

The camp swimming pool is 12 m long and 3 m wide. What is the area of the pool?   36 m²

Julio's math book is 10 in by 7 in. What is the area of his math book?   70 in²

With your child, measure the areas and perimeters of objects around the home, for example, the front of books, table tops, or doors. Measure the length and width and add to find the perimeter. Then multiply length and width to find the area.

Mass & Volume Problems ★

GOAL

Learn to solve problems about mass and volume.

Figure out the answers to these problems.

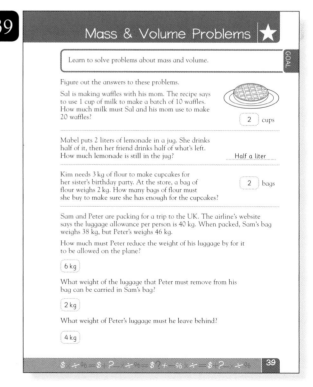

Sal is making waffles with his mom. The recipe says to use 1 cup of milk to make a batch of 10 waffles. How much milk must Sal and his mom use to make 20 waffles?   2 cups

Mabel puts 2 liters of lemonade in a jug. She drinks half of it, then her friend drinks half of what's left. How much lemonade is still in the jug?   Half a liter

Kim needs 3 kg of flour to make cupcakes for her sister's birthday party. At the store, a bag of flour weighs 2 kg. How many bags of flour must she buy to make sure she has enough for the cupcakes?   2 bags

Sam and Peter are packing for a trip to the UK. The airline's website says the luggage allowance per person is 40 kg. When packed, Sam's bag weighs 38 kg, but Peter's weighs 46 kg.

How much must Peter reduce the weight of his luggage by for it to be allowed on the plane?   6 kg

What weight of the luggage that Peter must remove from his bag can be carried in Sam's bag?   2 kg

What weight of Peter's luggage must he leave behind?   4 kg

When talking about mass and volume, it may be helpful to use empty food containers. Encourage your child to read the labels indicating the weight or volume, and then place the containers in order from the smallest to largest.

★ Telling the Time

GOAL Learn words and phrases that refer to the number of minutes when telling the time. For example:

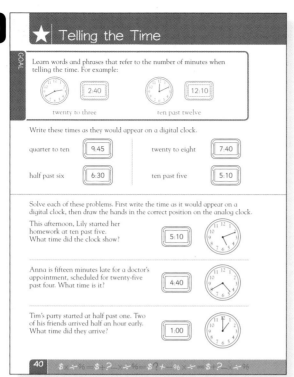

twenty to three | ten past twelve

Write these times as they would appear on a digital clock.

| quarter to ten | 9:45 | twenty to eight | 7:40 |
| half past six | 6:30 | ten past five | 5:10 |

Solve each of these problems. First write the time as it would appear on a digital clock, then draw the hands in the correct position on the analog clock.

This afternoon, Lily started her homework at ten past five. What time did the clock show? — 5:10

Anna is fifteen minutes late for a doctor's appointment, scheduled for twenty-five past four. What time is it? — 4:40

Tim's party started at half past one. Two of his friends arrived half an hour early. What time did they arrive? — 1:00

Young children are often confused by the many different ways of saying what time is it. Make sure your child is aware of the variety of different terms used when talking about time. Whenever you use a particular term, ask him or her to say exactly what it means.

Time Problems ★

GOAL Learn to solve problems about time.

Solve these problems. Write the times as they would appear on a digital clock.

Brianna left for her violin class at 2:45 PM. It took her 15 minutes to get there. After a one-hour lesson, it took her 15 minutes to walk home. What time did she arrive home? — 4:15 PM

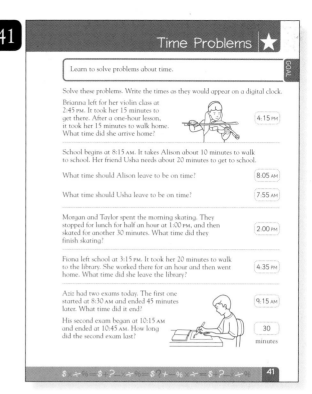

School begins at 8:15 AM. It takes Alison about 10 minutes to walk to school. Her friend Usha needs about 20 minutes to get to school.

What time should Alison leave to be on time? — 8:05 AM

What time should Usha leave to be on time? — 7:55 AM

Morgan and Taylor spent the morning skating. They stopped for lunch for half an hour at 1:00 PM, and then skated for another 30 minutes. What time did they finish skating? — 2:00 PM

Fiona left school at 3:15 PM. It took her 20 minutes to walk to the library. She worked there for an hour and then went home. What time did she leave the library? — 4:35 PM

Aziz had two exams today. The first one started at 8:30 AM and ended 45 minutes later. What time did it end? — 9:15 AM

His second exam began at 10:15 AM and ended at 10:45 AM. How long did the second exam last? — 30 minutes

Telling the time and estimating how long events and actions take are important skills. Your child needs to become confident in using these skills, both in everyday life and in order to move on to higher-grade activities.

★ More Time Problems

GOAL Learn to use a schedule.

To Midtown Stadium

From Greenport	Franklin	Midtown Stadium
9:15 AM	10:35 AM	11:50 AM
10:15 AM	11:35 AM	12:50 PM
11:15 AM	12:35 AM	1:50 PM

To Greenport

From Midtown Stadium	Franklin	Greenport
3:00 PM	4:15 PM	4:25 PM
4:00 PM	5:15 PM	6:25 PM
5:00 PM	6:15 PM	7:25 PM

Jenny and Fran are going to watch a tennis match tomorrow at the Midtown Stadium. Use the train schedule above to answer these problems.

The match begins at 12:15 PM. What time should Jenny take the train from Greenport to get to the stadium on time? — 9:15 AM

Fran plans to get on the same train at Franklin. What time is that train expected to reach Franklin? — 10:35 AM

After the match, Jenny and Fran leave the stadium at 4:30 PM. What time is the next train back to Greenport? — 5:00 PM

What time will Fran get off the train at Franklin? — 6:15 PM

What time will Jenny get off the train at Greenport? — 7:25 PM

Train schedules can often be difficult to read. Help your child gain an understanding of the schedules, their formats, and the time intervals shown. You could use copies of train schedules and play a game of questions and answers based on the information.

More Time Problems ★

GOAL Learn to read timelines. A timeline is a way of displaying events in the order in which they occurred, or in which you plan to do them.

Look at the timeline below that Carlo and Elda made to plan their work on a science project.

Monday	Wednesday	Friday
Look up information	Write report	Present project

Tuesday	Thursday
Search for pictures	Practice presenting project

Now use the information on the timeline to complete these sentences.

On Wednesday, they will write their __report__.

On Monday, they will look up __information__ to write their report.

On Thursday, they will practice __presenting__ their project.

On Tuesday, they will search for __pictures__ to illustrate their report.

On Friday, they will present their __project__ at the science fair.

Alice and her dad went to the Evergreen Harvest Festival. Here are some of the things they did there.
At 10:00 AM, Alice won a doll at a carnival game.
At 11:00 AM, Alice had her face painted to look like a cat.
At 12:00 PM, Alice and her dad ate cheese sandwiches for lunch.
Finally, at 1:00 PM, Alice and her dad bought a brownie to share.

Now write these events on the timeline below.

Alice won doll	Ate cheese sandwiches
10:00 AM	12:00 PM

11:00 AM	1:00 PM
Alice's face painted	Bought brownie

Learning to read timelines builds your child's confidence in reading schedules and provides a visual aid. Encourage your child to use a timeline when writing a book report or when developing a science or social studies project.

★ Pie Charts

Learn to read pie charts. A pie chart is a circular graph divided into sections. The size of each section represents the data for each category.

Students in Ms. Berry's class all love pies. This pie chart shows the kinds of pies they like best.

Types of Pie

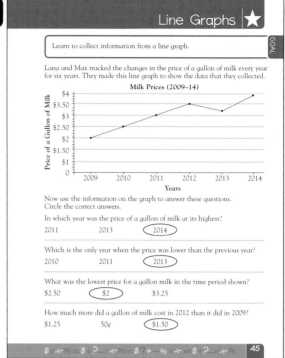

Blueberry 6
Apple 12
Peach 4
Banana 2

Now use the information on the pie chart to answer these questions.

How many children are there in Ms. Berry's class? **24** children

How many children in Ms. Berry's class like peach pies best? **4** children

How many more children like apple pie best than like peach pie best? **8** children

Which pie did most of the children say they liked best? _Apple pie_

Which pie did the fewest number of children like best? _Banana pie_

Which two pies did a total of ten children like best? _Blueberry pie and peach pie_

Discuss how information on a pie chart can be represented by fractions. For example, looking at the pie chart shown on this page, you could say that $\frac{12}{24}$ (or $\frac{1}{2}$) of the children in Mr. Berry's class like apple pie best, or that $\frac{6}{24}$ (or $\frac{1}{4}$) of the children like blueberry pie best, and so on.

Line Graphs ★

Learn to collect information from a line graph.

Lana and Max tracked the changes in the price of a gallon of milk every year for six years. They made this line graph to show the data that they collected.

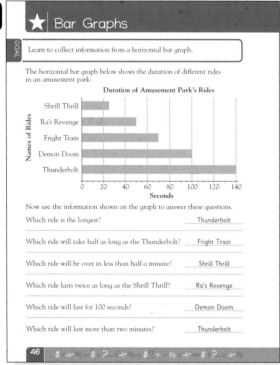

Now use the information on the graph to answer these questions. Circle the correct answers.

In which year was the price of a gallon of milk at its highest?
2011   2013   (2014)

Which is the only year when the price was lower than the previous year?
2010   2011   (2013)

What was the lowest price for a gallon milk in the time period shown?
$2.50   ($2) $3.25

How much more did a gallon of milk cost in 2012 than it did in 2009?
$1.25   50¢   ($1.50)

Explain that line graphs show how information or data can change over time. The price of milk, for example, can go up or down based on how much milk is produced and how many people buy it. If not enough milk is produced, less milk is available, and the price goes up.

★ Bar Graphs

Learn to collect information from a horizontal bar graph.

The horizontal bar graph below shows the duration of different rides in an amusement park.

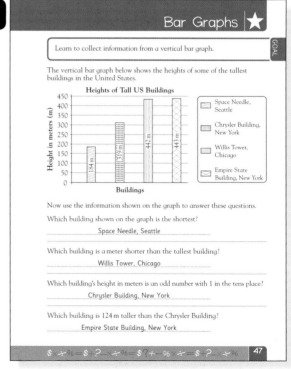

Duration of Amusement Park's Rides

Now use the information shown on the graph to answer these questions.

Which ride is the longest? _Thunderbolt_

Which ride will take half as long as the Thunderbolt? _Fright Train_

Which ride will be over in less than half a minute? _Shrill Thrill_

Which ride lasts twice as long as the Shrill Thrill? _Ra's Revenge_

Which ride will last for 100 seconds? _Demon Doom_

Which ride will last more than two minutes? _Thunderbolt_

Let your child create bar charts vertically and horizontally on graph paper. With him or her, list data on the fastest animals, popular sports, or perhaps favorite candy. Help him or her create the bar graphs, using a different color for each bar.

Bar Graphs ★

Learn to collect information from a vertical bar graph.

The vertical bar graph below shows the heights of some of the tallest buildings in the United States.

Heights of Tall US Buildings

Space Needle, Seattle
Chrysler Building, New York
Willis Tower, Chicago
Empire State Building, New York

Now use the information shown on the graph to answer these questions.

Which building shown on the graph is the shortest? _Space Needle, Seattle_

Which building is a meter shorter than the tallest building? _Willis Tower, Chicago_

Which building's height in meters is an odd number with 1 in the tens place? _Chrysler Building, New York_

Which building is 124 m taller than the Chrysler Building? _Empire State Building, New York_

Working with real data helps your child learn about the world, while also highlighting the importance of math and its connection with other subjects. Look up information about each building to give your child a frame of reference.